The Hand God Dealt Me

KAYAN SYKES

DR. NES INTERNATIONAL CONSULTING & PUBLISHING
Los Angeles County, CA

Kayan Sykes

© 2019 Kayan Sykes. All rights reserved.
Dr. Nes International
www.drnesintl.com

All rights reserved. This book, or parts thereof, may not be reproduced in any form, stored in any retrieval system, or transmitted in any form by any means – electronic, mechanical, photocopy, recording, or otherwise – without permission of the author, except provided by the United States of America copyright law or in the case of brief quotations embodied in critical articles and reviews.

The books recount certain events in the life of Kayan Sykes according to her recollection and perspective. The purpose of this book is not to defame, but to empower and motivate readers to face their challenges despite of pain and disappointment.

ISBN: 9781949461091

Editor: Sharp Editorial, LLC
Cover Design: Kavon Evans

Contents

Introduction 7

The Life Card 15
The Birth Card 33
The Parenting Card 63
The Unknown Man Card 71
The Trust Card 89
The Friend Card 93
The Race Card 99
The Dream Card 105
The Vegas Card 111
The End Card 123

About the Author 127

Kayan Sykes

Special Dedication

In loving memory of Mama Hicks, better known as Rosa Trice Hicks, a lady who gave me more than words could express. I remember every word she taught and everything she promised. Her love made me the person I am today. On my 15th birthday, I never imaged that day would be the last time she would say "Happy Birthday" to me. In my mind, I believed that Mama Hicks waited 'til the next day to go to sleep with the Lord, just for me. She couldn't stay another day on this Earth. Life changed, and I am forever grateful to God to have made it thus far, knowing she is watching over me until the day we meet again. Her many life lessons and the secrets she took to her grave, for the great acts of understanding, tending to my many needs, and showing me unconditional love are some of the main reasons I stand to tell my story. I love you, Mama Hicks, and I always will until the day I come to see you and the Lord.

The Hand God Dealt Me

Dedication

With every fiber of my being, I would like to dedicate this book to Jesus Christ, my Lord and Savior, the lover of my soul. If not for Him, I would be nothing at all. I have to say, without my mother, Elder Kenna Sykes-Harper, and her many days of prayer and standing before the Lord on my behalf, I would not know God. Her life has been a true testimony. This book is also dedicated to my mother's wonderful husband, Robert Harper, and all of his love and kindness. District Elder Kelvin Sykes is the man who raised me into the young woman I am today. Without the love and support of Lilly Fountain-Green, Kendall Sykes-Harvey, Sherdick Sykes, my grandparents, Doris Sykes-Fountain, Ulysses Sykes, and all of my cousins, this book would not be possible. Thanks to my sister/niece, Kyara Green, my go-to. To my prayer partner and cousin, Eva Sharif, I love you to life. To my many friends whom I can't name individually, I want to thank you for your love and loyalty. Most of all, I dedicate this book to my only son,

Kavon Evans. Without him, I would have never realized the true meaning of love. I see life in a different light because of him. I have come to realize that I owe you more than any mother could ever give. I love Kavon, second to God. Last but not least, I dedicate this book to Bishop Robby Owens, the man who showed me how to appreciate being a woman of God. His push for me to be all I could be, allowed me to truly open my eyes and "Go to the Mountaintop."

All of you are my world and the reason I live. Without your part in my life, I would have never made it to this point. God knows I love you.

Introduction

As I began to write this book, I faced many fears – a fear of not being fully understood by others, an admitted fear of judgment for my unique walk with God, and a fear that others may not understand just how deep I would express my truths to prove my point. I often wondered if I should allow others to step into my thoughts to understand the many ways God deals a hand of cards. He already has our lives planned and set into stone, and from my experience, I deal with these plans as if I see a deck of cards dealt directly into my hands. God is the card dealer, and I must trust my hand if I want to be on His team; I must follow the rules accordingly. I have read His Word, applied it to my life, and continually give God His Word back, the same Word He spoke throughout His commandments. I aim to follow these Biblical principles, step-by-step, to receive His many blessings while learning to play His game. I understand that life is not a game, so to speak, but this is a metaphor for facing the cards I was dealt. Some may believe differently, that life should not be compared to a game or deck of cards, but I believe that God has a sense of humor and He understands my message and intent.

As a child, others made decisions on my behalf which affected my life. Ultimately, those decisions led me to feel out of place everywhere I went. As a child, I had yet to realize that I had been handpicked by God who placed a huge, often unwanted call on my life before the foundation of the world had been created. I struggled to understand how I could be in so many difficult situations and overwhelmed by pain; however, I continued to love God with all my heart, acknowledging that He is the reason I am on this Earth to begin with.

When playing a game of cards, you are not permitted to speak a word about the game after the dealer deals your hand. You cannot talk to anyone around you, and you can't ask questions because, well, those are the rules. Plus, everyone else at the table has their own set of cards, so they are expected to do the same – deal with the cards they are dealt and not question the game or dealer. The rules of card games are similar to taking a test – the teacher does not talk to the student until the test is completely over, and then, and only then, will the teacher give the student a response or acknowledge their question.

God does the same sometimes, remaining quiet during the test, but with God, you will always come out on the winning side with clarity, understanding, and a deeper sense of faith.

Many people might wonder, "How is God a card dealer?"

Well, after you read this book, you will have a clear definition of this concept and metaphor.

Life has been designed for us to serve God and draw others to His love and kindness. In some churches, however, or when interacting with church folks, we never seem to see other hands of cards being played. Their hands are not revealed. We only see the side of them that comes to church, sits in the pew, and smiles as if they haven't been through anything but the right side of God. So, I want to take this opportunity to invite you to take a close glimpse at my hand so that you never feel alone, regardless of what you may be going through. I want you to understand that God's mighty power dictates our fate, and He deals multiple sets of cards to all of His children.

In this book, I provide a chance to become acquainted with my personal life for you to understand my point of view and my life from a different light. I welcome you to experience this ride and all of its twists and turns and, hopefully, you will develop the courage and faith to allow God to direct your every path, too. It took some time, but I grew to a place of deep faith, and I realize that having this understanding is better late than never.

It took 44 years for me to understand my purpose and run after my vision.

It took 44 years for me to love myself, enjoy life, and understand that God is in full control of everything, and if I continue to fall in love with Him, everything will work out just fine.

My choice to write this book was more difficult than you might imagine, but I knew, deep down, that I had the strength and courage to share these words with the masses. God gave me this assignment, and I knew I had to get this book done. I felt as though God was politely leading me in the direction of authorship, although His signs were more conspicuous than I'm used to. The first sign came when I was thinking about *not* writing this book. I was working at my desk when a woman approached me while I was writing on my notepad. I happened to be in deep thought as she walked by and asked, "Are you writing a letter?"

As I tried to cover my paper, she smiled and said, "That's a good thing. Never stop writing."

Shortly after this brief exchange, I had a deep discussion about life with a close friend, and midway through our conversation, she said, "KAYAN SYKES, you need to write that book!"

Those were two signs that I needed to put my pen to paper, but with the third sign, I couldn't help but feel as if He was talking directly through me. My friend and I went to church the following afternoon, and with a look in his eyes of pure Holy Ghost fire, the preacher suddenly said, "There is a book inside of you."

Several weeks after this sermon, I battled with thoughts about past relationships, business ventures, and a host of decisions I made in my past. As I went to visit the preacher's wife, I prayed she wouldn't see how flawed I thought myself to be. When I entered her office, she hugged me and softly said, "You have a story to tell that you haven't told anybody."

At that moment, I was flooded with emotions. Strangely, my tears remained guarded in my eyes, yet to roll down my face. My mind raced back to the many great people telling me to do something that God had been pulling on me to do. God had shown me clear signs in those brief moments, but fear of failure kept me from moving forward. After receiving His clarity and accepting His signs as deliberate nudges to write, I realized the time had come to tell my story.

God knows us more than we know ourselves; sometimes, He will send others to push us along our true path. Most of the time, the answers we are looking for are right in front of our faces. God will drop something in your heart, and if you truly listen and have a willing ear, He will give you exactly what you need. I often seek God, and I hear Him clearly, too, because my heart and mind are focused on His Word, His promise, and His Will for my life. His answer may not always be what I want, but I know His Word to be true. So, I continue to seek Him.

Thank you for taking the time to travel with me through my hand of cards. I hope my experiences propel you to own your truth, His Will for your life, and your inner strength.

Kayan Sykes

All blank pages are intentional

1
The Life Card

People have often wondered, "Who is Kayan Sykes. Lilly Nicole Sykes, the girl with the pretty face and great smile, the one who pushes through life and comes out victorious no matter what?" Despite others' positive perceptions of my life and identity, I've often felt unattractive and many times hated looking in the mirror. My grandmother used to say, "Kayan make sure you look nice at all times and keep your clothes together," but did she realize I was born to teenage parents, and I was bound to deal with internal and external struggles beyond the physical? Plus, my parents did not have a chance to pray over me in the womb, nor did they speak sweet nothings while carrying me. Still, my grandmother wanted me to make sure that I looked good at all times because that was of importance to her. Thankfully, my mother prayed over me and cuddled me once she learned to love God and cover me, and it was then that I was able to navigate through life without only worrying about one's outer appearance. Nevertheless, there are many lessons I've learned in this game of life. My mother was young when I was born, so my grandmother unofficially adopted me as her own, calling me her sixth child. This changed my life forever because no one ever imaged the role I would eventually play in my mother's life.

    Growing up, life was relatively normal until those moments came around when my mother, her brother, or my grandmother would get upset about one thing or another, and I would be tossed from side-to-side like a toddler playing with her dolly. If my grandmother were upset with my mother, they would exchange brutal words, and our home would turn into a war zone. This chaos was, at times, unbearable, and my stability was susceptible to shift due to their arguing. As life went on, Uncle Shedrick would always tell me that I'm in prison in my own mind.

Uncle Shedrick wasn't wrong, either, because I felt the same – mentally imprisoned. I felt lonely, unaware of who I was, often asking myself which card I should play that day. I pretended to be okay because my pride would not let anyone know I was anything other than happy. Nevertheless, those thoughts manifested and created equally imprisoned actions. Making friends was difficult for me, and my mother always commented about my perpetual unhappiness, yet I did not share what was truly going on in my mind or express my feelings regarding this card that God had dealt me.

I love my mother, and I always will, but we did not always see eye-to-eye. Little did she know, I was trying so hard to love her and honor her, and I wanted to be all that she desired for me. I've always believed my mother wanted me to be someone I wasn't because she just didn't understand me. She had me at a young age, and she did the best she could. I never needed or wanted for anything. She dressed me up like the little princess I wanted to be in my dreams. As my mother and grandmother continued to have their issues, my mother decided to grant my great-grandmother's wishes, allowing her to raise me instead of moving out of her home. She knew that moving would break my great-grandmother's heart. Despite this decision, we remained under the same roof. My grandmother worked while my great-grandmother cooked, cleaned, and made sure that everything my grandmother didn't handle stayed afloat. My great-grandmother ensured we were well taken care of. She was a firecracker, to say the least, despite her good intentions. However, the decision to remain under the same roof would inevitably rob my mother and me of the best times of our lives.

 God had a plan for us though, and regardless of what our lives looked like together, my mother and I certainly shared great times throughout our lives. Shopping created a bond for us, and if you know my mother, you know that shopping is her forte, aside from striving to be

God's best friend. She certainly lives up to her hype of being the best at praying and shopping. My mother is a bargain-queen, and finding great sales allows her to deal with her pain. She talks prices like nobody's business and will always reach Heaven if the prices aren't right, but when she prays, her words truly reach the hands of God. My mother taught me how to draw myself closer to God, and she gave her all when it came to her prayer life. I could not have had a better person praying for me. She didn't know what was going on inside my head, but she knew how to reach my heart in prayer. My mother would wake up at five or six in the morning, praying and speaking in all the tongues she could, seeking God to help me, and every morning, sure enough, my life would shift in a powerful way. She knows how to reach God, but the power of her prayer wasn't enough to change my card because God was and is in full control. Nevertheless, God's Word says that no weapon formed against me will prosper. I had to play this card called life to develop to the next spiritual level.

I have stories upon stories and memories upon memories of the women in my life, but not much to mention about my father. I remember one particular moment, clear as day, when I was four years old. I was walking up the black steel steps in the back of my cousin's house as my father walked down the steps from his sister's apartment on the third floor. As I passed him on the steps, he said something I will remember for as long as I live.

"She looks kind of like me," he said.

The rest of his words faded from my mind, just like my memory of him.

On my eighth birthday, my father's sister picked me up to spend some time together. My mother would often allow her to drop me off by our church and spend time with me because my grandmother forbid them to come to our house to see me. My father would hang out not too far from the church, and as I look back, I realize my aunt wanted him to see me. I assume she believed that my father would give me the "Happy Birthday" wish I had longed for. So, we exited her car and headed in the direction of my father's hangout spot. A few moments later, my father walked by me without a glance. He didn't care to take a look at me. With tears in my eyes and my aunt in sheer disbelief, we turned around and walked back to her car. That was the last time I saw my father in my early childhood years. I sat in the backseat of my aunt's car, closed my eyes, and tried to erase that moment from my mind, but as time progressed, I learned to understand how healing works. I realized that memories are good for your soul, even the painful ones. You have to open your mouth and let the memories that caused you pain to come out. In playing this card and accepting my emotions, I allowed God to be my Father.

    Fathers open car doors for their daughters.

    Fathers hold their children as they sleep.

    Fathers should be there to walk their children to their first class at school, and fathers should open the door before their child enters, showing the importance of having someone who teaches every lesson, big and small.

Fathers are also supposed to show their daughters a detailed example of how the man should play his part in her adult life.

All of these actions, positive reinforcements, and respectful behaviors show a young lady what to accept from others. Through my eyes, people treat you differently when you have a father in your life. I see life differently and believe I would have gone further, sooner, in an upward direction, if my father did his part, but I did not have my father to guide me or show me an example of what to accept from a man. Instead, I grew up searching for a man's love, care, and understanding in all of the wrong places, allowing myself to take whatever a man offered. This part of the card is something I have yet to understand fully, but on our walk with God, there will be lessons and circumstances that don't exactly make sense to us. Nevertheless, there is a purpose, and He has a reason for everything.

My father left me in the dark, but now that I have a better understanding of life, I realize that he couldn't give me something he did not have. A father should be there to support, to catch his daughter before she falls, and certainly to be there to listen to every problem. However, some fathers are unable to provide that level of support because that support is absent in their life, too. For the fathers reading this book, please pay close attention to the magnitude of my words and recollections and do your best to give your daughter everything she deserves.

I chose to rely on God, and He has been the Father I never had, yet I still wish I could've had my natural father in the earthly sense. God surely didn't disappoint, and He is always there. He has been better to me than I could ever be to myself. So, if you're having any type of problem, allow Him to come into your heart. He truly understands. He knows your pain, He knows your feelings, and He knows your next thought. Remember, He knew you before you were in your mother's womb (Jeremiah 1:5).

You must learn to trust God in your darkest hour. He is there to support and love you, and if you trust Him as your Father, He will turn your life around. For girls and women like me, we tend to hide in the fact that no biological father was there to guide us in the right direction, and although that may be true, God remains and always will be present. Sadly, however, we often move through life trying to find a man to replace our father so that this painful gap is not unfilled. Unfortunately, that method of replacement does not work well because God is the only Father that will make things right and complete. Without my biological father, I often blamed him for certain issues in my life, but I have come to realize that God allowed this absence. As a result of accepting this truth, I reached the joyous place I'm in today. As an adult woman, continuing in her development in the many areas of my fatherlessness, I understand that God does not always fix a situation the way you desire, but He teaches us how to cope and get through.

When I was a teenager, experiencing the emotional and physical changes that accompany adolescence, my best friends happened to be years older than me. I would go places and do things with them to seem older, assuming I could handle life on an older level. One Friday after school, my friends and I went to hang out with other older kids, and one particular guy asked me if I wanted to ride to the store with him. Of course, I agreed, but unbeknownst to me, he had something else planned. Before I knew it, he had pulled up to a house. He told me this home was his grandmother's, he had to pick something up, and I needed to come in with him. So, I got out of the car, visibly nervous that something wasn't right. Although my house was only a block away, I didn't think to run. Besides, I wasn't supposed to be with him anyway, and I didn't want to get in trouble. I entered the house with him, even after I saw him break the glass on the front door because he claimed he didn't have a key.

"Come in!" he loudly barked, pushing me up the stairs.

Kayan Sykes

With every step I took, a strong sense of fear took over, but I felt as though I couldn't turn back. He started to push me, dragging me down until I was on the couch in a dark, cold room. He pulled down my skirt while I struggled to keep it up, then forcing my panties to the ground. Then, he forced himself into me, and I felt every bit of pain, yet I was helpless. I couldn't do anything.

"I shouldn't have been with him in the first place," I softly cried as he continued assaulting me.

He finished his business, stood up, and whispered in my ear, "Don't you tell a soul."

At that moment, I didn't say a word.

I couldn't.

My heart was racing, and I just wanted to run far, far away.

I didn't know how to feel nor did I know what to say. I couldn't see straight. I just wanted to get back to my so-called friends who I thought would have noticed I was gone or worried that something terrible may have happened. Instead, they just went with the flow, hardly concerned that I had been gone for a while.

    That afternoon, I went home as if nothing had happened, but after a couple of days, the physical and emotional pain did not stop. I was afraid to express these feelings to my grandmother, and I believed that my mother would not understand. So, I called my mother's good friend whom I would often talk to about experiences at school and home. I would tell her my deepest fears and thoughts that I just couldn't get other people to understand. This time, however, I called her with a problem that was beyond my control and understanding. When she answered her phone, I began to get the words out, then asking her if she would take me to the hospital. I also asked her if she would tell my family because I knew I wouldn't be able to handle this alone. Between trying to force this memory from my mind, and the fact that many years had passed since his assault took place, I can't remember every detail of how this transpired, but I will never forget the responses of some of my family members.

That evening, my family arrived at my grandmother's house, just minutes away from where the rape had happened, and everyone gathered around the living room table after I made it home from the hospital. My grandmother's brothers, who were clearly not understanding nor wise at this time of my life, made hurtful, wildly inaccurate comments about my character. They felt as though I did this as an act of disobedience. Cleary, once again, I had been hurt by yet another set of male figures. I wasn't lying, and I was not a bad girl, but I was young and naïve, not yet realizing how many young women fall into the same trap that I did on that devastating afternoon.

"How in the world could this have happened to me?" I silently cried.

I pushed this situation to the back of my mind, yet repeatedly asked myself what was I to learn out of this man taking my most precious gift. As a young woman, I did not realize that I didn't deserve the pain I was going through, but that wasn't the last time I would experience physical and emotional trauma.

Shortly after the rape, I told my so-called teenage boyfriend.

"Let me make sure you were raped," he said, and I, being naïve, allowed him to force himself on me, now being raped twice by two different boys. This time, the rapist left a deposit, and at the age of fourteen, I was pregnant. There was no way my grandmother would allow me to bring a child into her house.

"You're not going to destroy your life with a baby," she said.

That afternoon, my grandmother phoned my aunt and said, "This child needs to be fixed."

So, we drove to a building in East Saint Louis. Upon entering, I noticed other young girls who were crying and looking at me as if they felt my pain. I walked to the receptionist's desk and gave my name. Less than ten minutes later, I was escorted to a small room that felt cold as ice. Feeling more afraid that my grandmother would hate me for the rest of my life if I went against her wishes,

I closed my eyes and held my breath as a man told me to remove my underwear. Then, an unbelievable pain jolted through my body. From that point forward, I refused to let my mind recall any more details from that dreadful day.

Hiding behind pain, I continued on with life, later having to tell my child-development teacher that I couldn't stay in her class because I heard a baby crying in my ears as she talked about parenting. Eventually, I dropped this class and did not discuss this part of my life for quite some time. This experience became the biggest secret of my life. Before this moment, I vowed that I would die before telling a soul, but I later realized that this pain had to be acknowledged, forgiven, and released. So, I gave it all to God.

If you have had a similar experience, please, I encourage you to drop the dead weight because every last pound is holding you down.

I forgave myself, and I forgave the men who hurt me. You should too!

Take it from me – forgiving yourself is the first step to a happy life. God's Word says to forgive 77 times (Matthew 18:22). There are 77 reminders in the Bible that you cannot allow the same people that hurt you to hold you back any longer. Releasing the pain feels so much better than holding on to it.

You are a winner, and your life was designed in victory. So, you must let go of the pain, anger, guilt, and resentment. I chose to release these feelings, once and for all, and I'm grateful to report that forgiveness was key in my healing process.

Kayan Sykes

2
The Birth Card

When I first laid eyes on my son, I suddenly forgot that his father was the man I met just days after getting a phone call from a friend telling me that my boyfriend was at the local pizza place with another girl. Feeling hurt from the news, I went to work and noticed this tall, handsome man walking down the hallway, a man I had previously known nothing about. All I could think was that I would love to have his baby and serve my current boyfriend a dose of his own medicine. Seconds after this wild thought, I asked myself, "What in the world has come over me?" Sleeping with another man wasn't going to only hurt my boyfriend, but it would change my life forever.

Looking in this little person's eyes made me forget that I was about to be a single mother, all alone, with no husband, no boyfriend, and no man to help parent, teach, and provide. Nevertheless, my child arrived four days before my 25th birthday. At the time, I was only concerned about my child having great looks, similar to the way my grandmother wanted me to take pride in my appearance, first and foremost. In retrospect, this level of importance became generational. Admittedly, my first concerns were not his health, intelligence, or priorities that a mother should have on her mind. In the beginning, I did not know how to embrace my son because I had other nonsense clouding my mind. I didn't realize he was a gift from God. As each moment went by, my motherly instincts started to kick in. My son was here, in my arms, and God had to be up to something because this beautiful baby was nothing short of a miracle. Looking down in his eyes as he latched on to my breast for a 45-minute feeding, he gently tugged on my soul and expounded my love, determination, honor, and all the kindness God has given me. All

I could think was that this card was going to do a lot for my life during a time when I had no idea how to love.

God set me up for that special moment.

While my son rested in my arms, I could feel the life that I had once given up on now climbing out my soul and entering into this little boy's being. I couldn't help but feel that every time he opened and closed his eyes, he was sending me a message that he was taking it all in and that he knew my love was growing and shifting. God will make an act of disobedience seem like magic as He reveals His purpose for your life, and this realization certainly felt magical.

As time progressed, my son reached various milestones. Upon saying his first words, he called me "Honey." I've looked this word up, many times, only to find that it means sweet, sticky, and someone who is dear, but I continued looking deeper and found a passage that stated, "Honey is someone that a person always needs, is very helpful regardless of the situation, and always gives a good laugh." As I began to think about everything, I experienced with Kavon, my son, up to this point, God revealed why he taught Kavon to call me such a great name at a young age. Through my child, I was going to have to grow into what God had in store for me, not knowing that it would fall into the plan God had for us both. I sought God's guidance on how to love Kavon and how to ensure my son would love me back. I wanted my son to look the part, I wanted him to do well in school, and I wanted him to be the best he could be in life. Most of all, I wanted him to make me proud. Backwards, I know, but at the time, those were my honest thoughts and feelings. I wanted people to say that I did a great job raising him alone. I wanted that satisfaction. I had yet to learn, however, that my purpose was not to be centered on my pride and desires.

    Just when I thought life was all about me and reaping all the credit, God changed my card. My beautiful son, whom I would soon discover had a mind of his own, also had an outgoing attitude at a young age and would tell people exactly what was on his little mind, every chance he had. He was a loving child to his family but was uncontrollable. Needless to say, school was a nightmare for me. He could pass tests without having to study, but he spoke out of turn. In preschool, after finishing his work, Kavon would tell his teachers he was done and ready to go home, knowing he had to finish his day. In his little mind, he was used to being in control, and this behavior carried on for years. Back then, I justified his actions as anything other than disrespectful, but his decisions would cause other children to join in with his controlling behavior, too. His teachers would get on him about talking back. In his defense, this behavior was my fault because I allowed him to speak his mind, and it was something that surely needed to be corrected. Raising Kavon around adults caused many issues. He was more advanced than his classmates, and although that doesn't exactly seem like an issue, it posed a problem in different situations. Kavon was an extremely bright child, yet he continued to do things that reminded us he was barely five years old. When he graduated from preschool, the time had come from him to walk across the stage. While on stage, he was asked what he wanted to be when he grows up.

"Jackie Chan!" he yelled.

I wanted to hide under my seat, but all I could do was love him to life. He was truly a handful at this age. As life continued, he would do things that made me run to the school or find myself on edge, hardly funny like the "Jackie Chan" comment. Oh my goodness, the stories I have about Kavon! I was surely earning the name he had been calling me, Honey, but as I played my card, I kept fighting for him. Like many parents, however, I was not always doing what was right. I often felt the need to defend myself when it came to parenting Kavon. I would remind others that I was never given a handbook or directions on how to raise my son. I went with what I thought was right, and God knows all I could do was do things the way I felt my mother did which was pray and cry out to God to show me the way. I wasn't a Bible scholar or a great saint, but I knew how to pray. I cried so many tears in those days because I felt that God had put this unfamiliar responsibility on my shoulders. I did not have a clue about how to handle my child, and I did not know how to harness and develop all he had to offer the world. I blamed myself for Kavon's fatherless situation, feeling that my life without my father was repeating itself and my child would have some of the same issues. Nevertheless, I knew this was something I got myself into, and although I would cry or try to shift blame, this ultimately rested on my shoulders.

Putting Kavon through school was difficult. I fought with myself and everyone at his school because I believed he was not challenged nor given the care I thought he needed. I felt that it was easier for the school staff to punish him or tell me that he needed something to calm him down in the form of a pill rather than find a method to help this child that had been tested as gifted. I would become upset and leave town with friends, dragging Kavon from school to school and city to city, but situations would unfold beyond my liking which drew me right back home to Saint Louis until I would get upset and venture out again. Once, I decided to move to Texas and deal with life on my own. This decision led me to face life from a very different perceptive. Kavon and I drove more than 1,000 miles, only to sleep on the floor of one of my former hair clients whom I had previously become friends with in Texas. She moved from Saint Louis and sold me a dream that would move me to having false hope. It wasn't the greatest situation, as I initially thought it would be. When we first moved in, she told me not to sit on her new couch for too long, forbidding us to sleep on the couch at night. At the time, I received food stamps. So, I was using those food stamps to buy groceries and cooking for all of us, but she would get mad and tell me not to eat all the food I was buying. Finally, I asked God to get me out of this situation. Sure enough, my Father did it again. This time, we slept at the home of one of my mother's friends. One afternoon, my mother's friend had called and said, "Come over, child, and sleep in the bed. I will get you an airbed in the morning."

That night, we ate, took a bath, and had the best sleep we had in a long while. God showed Himself in this card, revealing yet again that He will create a way, and He had His human angels providing for me.

As I recall these memories, tears fill my eyes, burning in remembrance of how I've been made to feel throughout my motherhood card. The Word of God says not to have a child out of wedlock, and I have always wondered if my life's circumstances were a punishment that many other single women feel, too. Despite my pain and the devil's taunting thoughts, I held on to God and never gave up, and I remembered that my mama would pray that her seed would be mighty on this Earth. I had to work and trust that God would protect Kavon, my seed.

With tears streaming down my face, I left my then nine-year-old son at home as he got himself together for school while I talked to him from my desk at work at 4:30 am. I would get home by 1:00 in the afternoon and, thankfully, God had His angels to watch over our things until I arrived home. I was now in my own apartment, and my new job was finally getting me from Point A to Point B. I took many risks while trying to be the best mother I could, all while dealing with so much pain and discomfort.

After managing to live in Texas for 18 months, I decided to move to Las Vegas to reunite with an old boyfriend, thus dragging my baby from a stable situation with the thought that God said I could leave again. Leaving Texas and eventually crossing into Nevada, my son and I rode down the highway, singing and talking. Although the moment seemed joyful, quiet tears rolled down my face because I realized that I did not know what I was getting ready to experience. My previous boyfriend had moved to Vegas and, in my heart, I hoped he would drive my unwanted problems away. Thankfully, God's angels encamped all around us through the mountains and hills until we ended up at the in Prim Valley Resort, 45 miles outside of Las Vegas. I landed a job but would have to drive Kavon 50 miles to school so no one would report a minor alone in a hotel room while I worked downstairs in the lobby. On the weekends, we stayed in one hotel, only to eat and bathe. Kavon was only in school for 45 days when I was dealt another difficult card.

My car was repossessed.

Not knowing where to turn, I found myself on a 30-hour bus ride back to St. Louis with nothing but my son and his clothes, leaving all of our other belongings behind. During this bus ride, I realized we were leaving everything and starting over once again.

All I could do was pray.

I can't say that God didn't give me a warning not to go. You see, the very day I left Texas, I had a friend at my place, and she was on the phone with a woman who I had never laid eyes on and never had spoken to either. During their conversation, the woman said, "Tell your friend she shouldn't go. Tell her to wait. God is saying 'not yet.'" But me being me, I convinced myself otherwise. My great-grandmother, Mama Hicks, would always say that a hard head will make a soft behind, and I found this to be true throughout life. God will send warnings, but it's up to you to listen. So, I landed myself right back in St. Louis after this incident in Vegas. This time, I had to live with my grandmother, and Kavon and I had no choice but to catch the bus wherever we went.

Kavon was enrolled in another school, yet again, and as I looked at the children in this public school that I was forced to put Kavon in, I noticed that many of these children came to school hungry and not having proper clothes for the weather. I asked myself, "God, how in the world did I get in this position? How did I allow myself to go from having it all to riding the bus and having no job and no home?"

Still, I loved God with all my heart. I knew He would come through, emotionally, mentally, and financially. However, I still had to learn how to make better decisions.

The anger inside of me made me determined to work harder, and I realized I had to start listening to Him and following His directions. I had to come to grips with myself, accepting that I needed to take a step back and stop running from the truth. I had to accept my problems, deal with them, and vow never to give up or turn away from His Word. The days and weeks went by, and Kavon and I eventually moved into a sublet apartment in Chesterfield, Missouri. Still not having a job, I managed to do enough hair and sell enough candy to pay the rent and get a car. The struggle of being on my own and not having enough money was real, but no one knew what I was going through. I kept my hair together, and my outward appearance was polished, but the pain of starting over was eating me up inside. I was fighting to stand above water to handle these life issues.

Two months after Kavon's 14th birthday, I had to play yet another difficult card which would change our lives and nearly take the breath from my body. Before this terrible incident, I had become the Praise Team Leader at our church. I was praying on Thursday nights, leading the opening Prayer for Life class, and singing before the Pastor entered the pulpit every Sunday. I was giving God all I had. My life was devoted to Him, and everyone around me could see the life change I had made. I was like a newborn Christian; my walk was different, my talk was different, and I was a different person, inside and out. Nothing could bring me down or stop me from doing God's Will in the church, the same place I once called my napping spot.

 I began leading and organizing different avenues of the church with my uncle, stepping into a position that caused other family and church members to dislike me. In my heart, I always felt that this newfound leadership role caused my uncle's wife to look at me in a very unfriendly way. Nevertheless, my heart was in the right place, and church had become everything to me. Kavon learned to play the keyboard, too. I had never prayed for him to become a musician, but God was using him, and life was on a good path. I often allowed Kavon to go to my uncle's house to spend the night. My uncle was the pastor and the man who raised me with my mother. He was the acting father in our lives. Throughout my life, he has been so good to me, although we've had our issues like any family relationship. Nevertheless, he was the only man I trusted with Kavon. In fact, he was the person that rushed me to the hospital when Kavon forced his way into the world. We had a bond that no one could break, or so I thought. We kept each other's secrets, laughed together, and cried together. I was his biggest fan, and he was surely mine, too. My uncle's children would stay at my apartment as if it belonged to my uncle himself. They occupied a place in my heart as if they were my real brothers. I was my uncle's right-hand man, and I was grateful for this stage of love, trust, and stability. Many days, I would say to myself, "This man was building something that would save me from all my worries, next to God, and I honor him dearly."

On Father's Day of 2015, I prepared dinner for him and invited all of his children and family to my friend's house, and we enjoyed one of the best dinners to date. The evening was unbelievably amazing. We were among good company, we enjoyed good food, and the energy among everyone was joyous.

The following Monday, I received a call that my only son, Kavon, had been hurt and was in the hospital.

"But he's with my uncle! What could have happened? How did this happen?" I questioned, thinking that this is the call no mother ever wants to receive.

I ran out of my job as fast as I could and sped down the road, praying to God to cover my baby. Not knowing what had happened, still miles from the hospital, it seemed as if the highway was getting longer as my car floated across the lanes. By the time I arrived, I had jumped out of the car and noticed blood all over my child. No one was there with him. No one was in sight to explain what had happened to Kavon.

He was alone.

I wondered about my uncle's whereabouts, the same uncle I trusted to be by his side that

Sunday evening. Running to the front of the ambulance, I immediately saw the tears in Kavon's eyes.

"Honey," he breathed, "I'm okay. The blood isn't mine."

I couldn't believe my eyes. I could hear the noise around me, but I could not understand anything that was happening. My child was hurt, and although the details of this situation are lengthy, I am legally unable to discuss what had taken place. Nevertheless, Kavon was hurt, and I had no idea who had done this to him. No one was talking to me. Cops were scattered about everywhere, yet I couldn't get anyone to give me answers.

Suddenly, an officer turned to me and said, "You can't take him with you."

"I can't take him with me?" I questioned, not knowing who did this to my child or how this happened.

"Lord, what am I going to do?" I silently cried.

At that moment, all I could hear was that I was not permitted to take Kavon with me.

This situation was painful from many different angles. My son was hurt, I was confused and overwhelmed with unanswered questions, and I had to deal with this horrible situation alone, a painful reminder of my ongoing emotional struggles. This felt like a horrible nightmare, yet I was convinced I would wake up any minute. Needless to say, this was not a nightmare. Instead, it was the longest night of my life. I had to watch my child grimace in pain as the doctors told the police that they would have to transport him to a children's hospital. I chased behind the police car, driving and thinking, crying out to God. I drove as if no one else was on the road, clearly unconcerned about the police in front of me.

Upon approaching the hospital, I walked next to Kavon's rolling bed as he remained in handcuffs. Still, no family member in sight. When I realized I couldn't cry any more tears, Uncle Kelvin appeared in my peripheral. To this day, I can't remember what he said, but I knew there was nothing he could do at this point. He couldn't fix this, and I had to deal with the repercussions.

The Hand God Dealt Me

Kavon needed surgery, so after the doctors put his broken wrist back into place, the time had come for me to say goodbye to my only child who had never been away from me for longer than an evening. Not knowing what was going to happen, I felt as though I would never be the same and he would never be the same, too.

This card was one of the hardest cards I had to play and, at the time, I was convinced I would never make it through this ordeal.

The police officers escorted Kavon to a juvenile holding place for boys, and I was told I could only see him on Tuesdays and Sundays, in person yet via phone, for 15 minutes each visit. I had never been away from Kavon for any reason other than an overnight stay, and our lives immediately seemed to shift into a direction that felt painfully unfamiliar. As God allowed me to play this card, I had to trust Him in a way I had never trusted before.

There were days when the fear of losing my son took over my mind and body, and in those moments, I would pray to God to watch over him and protect him from seen and unseen dangers. I really did not know what my next step should be, but I trusted God so much that I found myself talking to Him every second of the day. My daily discussions with God gave me understanding that a mother's love for her child runs so deep that life is expected to exist in a constant state of change.

Motherhood is something that scared me throughout my entire life. Actually, I did not want to have a child because I believed I would be the worst mother in the world, but God showed me how to be a Godly mother, and I put my entire life into this blessed role. In my many prayers and conversations with the Lord, I questioned, "God, how could You deal me this hand, a hand that would destroy me and tear my family apart?"

I prayed through my anger and tears, sometimes finding clarity and peace, and other times being met with more anger. Nevertheless, no matter how I felt, I continued to look inward and prayed to the one and only God I knew would deliver me from these feelings of confusion, sadness, and anger. Although my prayer life remained strong and intact, I could not look at my uncle or his kids. The anger I felt for my family was beyond my wildest imagination.

During the first night away from my son, I sat on the floor of my Valley Park apartment and cried countless tears, truly feeling the weight of the world on my shoulders.

God, why?

What did I do, God?

I love my child.

I'm sorry for ever saying I didn't want him.

I love him.

I'm sorry for all my sins!

Thought after thought and emotion after emotion ran through my mind and exited my mouth. Whatever I felt, I shared with God, and in this constant state of prayer, I managed to blame myself, 100% percent, for everything that transpired. I replayed everything in my head, cursing at myself for allowing Kavon around these people in the first place. The anger, rage, and back-and-forth battle in my head were overwhelming, and I knew that my child was too good for this mayhem. This ordeal is why I moved him away from everything in the first place, so that I could avoid potential pitfalls and drama. I wanted Kavon to be safe, feel safe, and live a good life, yet there we were, in a situation I prayed we would never face.

That night was one of the longest nights of my life, and there was nothing to do except talk to God. I was unable to take off work. I mean, bills had to be paid, and I had to maintain a roof over our heads, yet I had no idea what was happening to Kavon while he stayed at the detention center. As frightening as the unknown can be, I had no other choice but to go on with life.

Similar to the days of my adolescence, I was yet again smiling on the outside while crying on the inside, but this time around, I learned to trust God on a deeper level. Dealing with the pain of failure, I stayed to myself while hiding behind the pain I continued to push away. In time, as I stuck with my full-time job, I earned back my car, purchased clothing, and continued to elevate, realizing that no one knew what was really going on in my private life. Financial stability was the one bright light in my life, and staying financially afloat kept me going, knowing that I was creating a solid environment for my son for when he returned home. I held on to God and pleaded with Him to keep my spirits strong. Growing up in church, I knew how to pretend to praise God while wanting to die inside, and although this is certainly not a healthy coping method, I was not yet ready or willing to let people into my emotional journey. I didn't talk to many saints, so people at church merely assumed I was out of town, not realizing I was hiding from the world, but the time would eventually come that I couldn't hide anymore.

To this day, I am legally unable to speak about the situation in full detail, but just know that Kavon's ordeal was one of the most horrible times of our lives. Nevertheless, through the pain, the unfamiliar, and the devastation, I trusted God, and that is a beautiful piece of my testimony. Placing my full trust in Him was hard, but

I learned to always put God first and trust Him with everything. I understand that God gave us a testimony and a horror story at the same time. I learned that trusting in God's Will does not mean you are free from anger or that He expects you to be happy at all times. In fact, I know that God understands our anger, and He wants us to give it all to Him, the good and the bad. In my moments of anger, I cried out to God that I gave my life to Him, I went to church every day, and I changed my life for the better, so why did this happen to us. I questioned why He let this happen to me, to us. I made Kavon my everything, and our mother-son relationship was genuine and honest. Elements of pride and selfishness exited my life long ago and were replaced with joy, selflessness, and humility. I was proud to be a mother, and I was a proud protector, provider, and role model, yet I could not take my son out of this mess, and it hurt like hell.

Finally, a small voice inside my head whispered, "I love Kavon, and he is going to be a great man."

At that moment, tears streamed down my face, and I cried harder than ever. Memories started flooding my mind, and I remembered that what my mother said: "This boy is going to be a great man of God." As I cried, I remembered God's Word: "I will never leave you or forsake you." So, I went to work, every day, with red eyes, and I had lost a great deal of weight in a short span of time. The phone calls stopped from many of my close friends and family, yet my walk with God grew stronger; He was all I had. I would reluctantly drag myself to that place, the detention center, to see Kavon, a place that no one wants their child to be. I'd smile on the outside to show my son I was strong for him, but my heart was bleeding with pain. I told God that I trusted Him and loved Him, and if He worked this out, I would serve Him even more, but no matter what happens, I would continue to give Him my all.

This was a 45-day test of faith, but a miracle finally came to pass. After Kavon's trial, my son was released, and the truth had set him free, but the pain lingered in various regards. This ordeal became the issue in our lives that my family would need God the most to keep us together. My uncle, who I loved more than my own father, could not understand my son's incident had choked away my life. I had to make a decision that would only draw me closer to God and further from my uncle, the man I believed would be in my corner forever.

During this time of painful confusion, the thoughts in my head got so out of hand that I lost focus on what God was saying. I could not hear or feel anything but the hurt and pain I had endured from Kavon's situation. Even though God had worked things out, and Kavon was finally home, I became so full of fear that I was always on edge.

God performed a miracle, yet I could not move past my lingering pain and debilitating thoughts. It was like I was moving backward, and as I regressed, I became angry with God. I loved Him, but I could not believe He could open one door for me yet close my heart to people, too. I started to grow cold and distant from the church. I just could not deal with the pain, so I found myself missing in action. I stopped singing and praising, and as I put my spiritual life on hold, I started to watch my child turn into someone else. We went from having amazing conversations and tons of laughs to barely exchanging words.

"I just want to be left alone," he would mumble.

I was mad at life, and within a matter of days, I turned into someone else. The family I had once worshipped with every Thursday night and Sunday morning had become distant and cold. I became even more lost, yet I knew and felt the love of God deep in my heart. Eventually, several years later, my mind clicked with my heart, and I understood the importance of sharing my feelings instead of running from my emotions, no matter how overwhelming. In a drastic turn of events, I began sharing my story with everyone. I just wanted to get this weight off of my chest. More and more, I found myself talking to others. During this breakthrough period, Kavon started a new job, and he picked up the pieces to his life as if nothing ever happened. Although I was proud of his progression, I also knew that ignoring the past, such a significant part of our lives, was not the best thing to do to achieve long-term healing. I prayed for Kavon, daily, and in praying for my son, I learned to heal, too.

Prayer

Lord, I believe you love Kavon, and I love him with all my heart, too. God, you know the things that I can't see, and I trust You to lead and guide him along the way. God, please heal him from his secret hurt; please take away whatever is deep in his heart and make him better. God, I trust that You have Your angels right beside him, coming and going. Lord, please whisper sweet nothings in Kavon's ears. God, he is my only child, yet I know he was Yours first. You formed Kavon while he was in my belly, and for that, God, I trust You. God, I know You have his beginning to his ending planned out, and I trust You with my son. I will rest in You on his behalf.

A man now stands where my baby used to be, and the sight of him all grown up moves me. My son is becoming wiser and stronger as the great man I want him to be. God, thank You for blessing him, day after day. I'm pleading with You to give him favor with everyone he comes into contact with. I want him to have Luke 22 buried into his heart. In Jesus' name, Amen!

I recite that prayer to this very day. God heard my cry, even through my hurt and pain, and I continued to believe in Him despite my quieted spirit. I have always said that I don't understand God, but I trust Him in so many ways. Kavon has grown, and God is working things out. We managed to move past that situation, and other situations which have come up as well, and I have learned so much about my child, too. Through this situation, God has allowed us to see Him in so many new ways, and we've been blessed by a fresh beginning and new chapter. God is not finished with us yet, and we are determined to finish the race God has set before us. Life is not easy, and we may not understand everything God has us endure and experience, but the reward will come, and the pain will subside. One day, Kavon will tell his own story, and when sharing his story, I know he will give God the glory for the hand he was dealt.

3
The Parenting Card

Some may wonder what parenting looks like in the eyes of God. Proverbs 22:6 states, "Train up a child in the way he should go, and when he is old, he will not depart from it." Then, Ephesians 6:4 states, "Fathers, don't provoke your children to anger, but bring them up in the discipline and instruction of the Lord." Also, Proverbs 13:24 states, "He who spares the rod hates their children, but the one who loves their children is careful to discipline them." I've always said that parenting is something that we learn as we go, and many times, we want our children to do things differently. As I researched the scripture, I had a misunderstanding about parenting until God dealt me the motherhood card. As a new mother, I initially felt that we never received instruction, but, in fact, we do.

While some follow and some do not, the instructions are in His Word.

Furthermore, the Lord knows the enemy will enter our parenting picture, yet He shows us how God truly loves us and how He must teach and guide us, too. The devil will try to sway our children, but by the instruction of God, He will help our kids to develop a life of prayer. If we do not take heed to His corrections, we will make decisions outside of His Will and never learn the lesson at hand. How many times do we look at our children and say, "Your attitude is bad" or "I didn't listen to my mother when she told me the same thing"? Our children will mirror who we were as children. God gives us our children to have and raise, and while we play this card, we must realize that God is the ultimate parent. Once you follow His instructions and learn the rules according to God's handbook, you will win. You will learn to move when and how God instructs. God will allow us to move at our own pace, but as soon as you step out of line, He will direct you right back into place, if you learn to listen and humbly follow. If you learn to listen the first time around, you will spare yourself the pain and frustration of repeating your mistakes. Children learn to live by example. So, if you have an active prayer life, your children will, too.

I've always said that our children will suffer if we, the parents, do not listen to God. Although my mother was not perfect, she trusted God's Will. Had it not been for her, I would have endured so much trouble. My mom and I may not see eye-to-eye on everything, but I give her all the credit for praying to God to cover me. Look at yourself and ask, "Are the troubles my children face on account of my refusal to live a life of God?" There are times we must face our rebellion, pride, and foolishness and realize that our indiscretions are affecting our kids, too.

Initially, Kavon and I did not have the picture-perfect mother-son relationship. Throughout his early childhood years, I did not know how to parent him properly, and I was not reading the Word like I should have been. I knew right from wrong, and I tried my best to make sound decisions, but I realized that I wanted him to be my best friend more than I wanted a son. In fact, I could not stand to discipline him. I did not want him to cry, so I gave him whatever he wanted, and as we all know, nothing particularly great comes from spoiling your child to death. "For the moment, all discipline seems painful rather than pleasant, but later it yields the peaceful fruit of righteousness to those who have been trained by it" (Hebrew 12:11).

There came a time when I thought I lost all control over Kavon. I would run to his rescue whether he was wrong or right. I took up for him, no matter the case, and as time went on, our loving relationship went south. I mean, I never set boundaries; we had no rules, and the truth is, all children crave structure and rules, no matter how much they may fight it or rebel. In retrospect, I understand the importance of boundaries and discipline, yet my realization came too late in Kavon's life.

There was one lesson I did stress, however, and that was never to lie. I would often say that a liar can't tarry in the sight of God, and this rule was about the only principle I would stand on. I did not want to be that parent who coddled my child for everything, but because of my issues at hand, that's exactly the parent I became. I would push Kavon to do his best, and I made sure he looked presentable, but there were lessons and rules I failed to instill, but by the grace of God, He showed me how to turn my parenting approach around. First, I had to heal from not having my father and not having the mother-daughter relationship I always wanted. I had to acknowledge these truths, face them, and finally put them behind me rather than carrying this toxic weight into my relationship with Kavon.

"God, show me the way," I cried out.

Facing the depths of my pain was excruciating, but I remembered a lesson my uncle had taught during one particular life class. He told us that God would sometimes hurt us to help us. At the time, I did not understand the magnitude of this lesson, but as I faced my feelings, I soon understood the meaning of being a parent. It hurt like hell to let my only child go through certain ordeals without holding his hand and to develop into a man right before my eyes. God is still helping me along my journey of positive and productive parenting.

If you want to develop a change in your relationship with God and your children, you must allow God to fix the broken pieces of your heart. I am not in the least finished with playing this card, but this is one card that God is making easier to play every day. If God is helping me work through my pains, stressors, and weaknesses, He can surely help you, too.

The Hand God Dealt Me

Prayer

Heavenly Father, thank You for parenting me. Thank You for trusting me with my child's precious life. Please teach me to follow Your instruction for my life. Thank You for not sparing the rod in my life, for without You, I would be lost. God, I want to thank You, once again, for my child, and I ask that You help me to lead him in the right direction. I give him back to You, over and over, and I allow You to parent him so that he can walk upright before You, oh God. Protect him, God, and show him how to play his cards right before Your sight! In Jesus' name, Amen.

Kayan Sykes

4

The Unknown-Man Card

Four years ago, I wanted to meet someone smart, loving, and kind, and although I never imagined how this would unfold. My gosh, life has been one hell of a ride. One night, just a couple of days before the fourth of July, I signed up online to potentially meet a new man. I remember this evening like it was yesterday. An older man had contacted me to chat, and at the same time, I wondered what in the world I was doing on this site. At that moment, I remembered that I had previously gone to a wedding of a woman who found her mate online, that my mother had a friend who was using the same site as me, and my little cousin often dated online, too. So, I convinced myself that online dating couldn't be that bad.

"Kayan Sykes, what are you going to find?" I asked myself and chuckled.

I looked at a couple of profiles and thought that a few of the prospects were too young, cute but young, and some looked a bit crazy, too. After coming across a number of much older men, people I did not consider dating, I logged off, convinced that this attempt at dating was not sent by God.

I always thought that a woman's future husband is supposed to find her sitting somewhere looking cute or find her praising God in church and say that he's been looking for her all her life. Then, of course, I pinched myself and woke up from that dream.

"Girl, get real," I'd laugh to myself as my mind replayed that daydream, over and over again.

Despite my strange experience with browsing this online dating site, I decided to give it another try. This time, I logged in, and an older white man messaged me.

"Really, God? Really?" I mumbled to myself, questioning why this man reached out to me.

Nevertheless, I was bored and lonely, and I figured I had nothing else to do. So, I responded, and this man talked my ear off about God and the plans God has for me.

"You're going to find someone, but that someone isn't me," he said.

I laughed, vowing to myself to never tell anyone about this.

Then, I got another hit from a guy who seemed into church life. He seemed friendly, but not exactly my type in the physical sense. Still, I give our conversation a shot, all the while thinking that I totally lost it for being on this site in the first place, but hey, my phone wasn't ringing with men, so I figured I didn't have much to lose. Then, this joker hits me with, "You know, I don't feel that God sent you as my wife."

Ouch.

In a span of two days, I had been dumped by men I had never even seen. This card I was playing was playing me because I wasn't getting any hits. I was dressing up, taking pictures, and posting them on these sites, but nothing was digging me except the devil.

"This is all a mistake," I said aloud. "I need to focus on God and leave online dating alone," I affirmed.

One night, my grandmother came to my house to spend some time with me. During this time, I had made up my mind that I was done with looking to be found; however, I kept the dating app on my phone but decided not to log in and participate... but then something happened. I received a notification that I had a message.

"God, if this is of You, it will work out," I quietly said.

I checked out the profile of this particular messenger and immediately noticed that this guy was cute! So, I accepted his request. Feeling nervous about giving my number out, I decided to send a couple of messages before exchanging digits. As I sat in excitement, my phone finally rang and, of course, I did not answer on the first ring. I waited until the third or fourth ring before answering, and in my cutest voice, I answered my phone. Meanwhile, I was laughing on the inside and thanking God at the same time because I hadn't heard a man's voice in a while. The man on the other end of the phone had the most perfect, warm, and soothing voice. Through conversation, I discovered he was a God-fearing man, and he knew so much about God, the church, and everything that faith had to offer. That night, we talked until the late hours of the day.

    Our conversations continued for several days, and with each talk, I would tell him I wasn't interested in dealing with a man in his position, one who was in a leadership role at the church. The men in leadership roles in the church, whom I had heard about from other women, apparently had issues, none of which I felt were worthy of my time. I let this new gentleman know off the bat that I just wanted a man who was willing to get to know God in the way I did. I wanted a man who would fall in love with God and understand how to love me through the love of God. As I told him everything I wanted in a man, he would just say, "Okay, Kayan, I got you." We would talk for hours each night, and he would call me when I made it home from work to hear about my day. He would listen to my sweet nothings, and in my heart, I felt that he had to be the one sent from God.

After several nights of talking on the phone, we decided to meet face-to-face. He would often say he had a couple of things he needed to tell me about himself, and each time he said that I would say, "Oh, trust and believe, I have a crazy past about myself, too," never realizing that his walk with God had been closer than I ever imagined. His life was one that many wouldn't understand, and that is what piqued my interest in meeting him. One's past has never been something I was afraid of because I figure we all have something that God had to work out of us.

I wanted a real man.

I wanted someone who was honest with me about everything.

I wanted someone to rescue me from the hurt my family had caused.

I wanted someone to fill the void of not having my father watch over me.

I wanted someone to hold me tight and tell me that all my problems were going to go away.

As I spent some time thinking about what I wanted in a man, I realized I wanted a king, but was this card the right card or was God dealing me a joker?

On the night we decided to meet, I put on my best pair of jeans and a blouse that made me look petite, and my hair and makeup were flawless. I had enough courage to pull this off, and I swore to myself that this was going to be my time to shine. As many may not know, "shy" is my middle name, and "fear" was often my last, but not that night. I had nothing more to lose, and I was ready to step out on hope and leave my fear behind. I had been single for six years, and if God allowed me to meet this man, then I knew I should not keep waiting for another opportunity to present itself. I decided to let go of the pain from past relationships and embrace what could potentially be a match made in Heaven.

Truth be told, my first marriage was not a success.

Oh, yeah, that.

I was married.

This relationship is not something I try to keep in the forefront of my mind. Simply put, it was a big failure, one that I did not care to share in the previous chapters. I figured since I had a failed marriage at the age of 22, and I birthed a child at the age of 25, then I believed that at 40 I could take a chance with a guy whom I met online. Laughing at myself, I said, "God, just take the wheel. This should be a walk in the park."

The time had come to meet this man for our date. My heart was racing as I drove down the highway to our destination. Thanks, unto God, I managed to pull myself together before I got to the parking lot where we had previously discussed meeting. I looked in my rearview mirror for what seemed like the 100th time, but I still did not see his car. I sat for a couple of minutes longer, thinking he was failing my first test of being on time, until he finally pulled into the lot... but I could see a lady inside the car with him. I looked away as he parked, trying to go unnoticed. I opened my door and slowly stepped out. As he turned around, our eyes met. He walked my way, and I could feel my heart pounding in my chest as I opened my mouth to say hello. The word came out as a mere whisper. Then, I managed to say, "I'm Kayan, how are you?" His eyes checked me out from head to toe, and then he said, "Hello. Come this way, and by the way, this is my attorney, Josephine. She is here as a friend."

"Who is this fellow, and why does this nig have his lawyer on our first date?" I wondered, then forcing myself to focus and give this a shot.

Having no clue as to what was going on, I continued to follow him into the building. We sat down, and I discovered that he was more than I expected. He told me about his past life and more about his line of work as a devoted preacher, but I never imagined our date would have been this eventful. There were so many thoughts going through my mind, but at this point, I was grateful that he was employed and owned a car. Finally, a man I wouldn't have to help.

"Jesus," I thought, "This is a man I can count on and maybe get some help from, too," I thought.

After this night, we continued dating, and I began to like him more and more. He wasn't tall and light-skinned like I normally liked my men, but he was a handsome man with light brown eyes that took me in and warmed my entire body. The more he talked to me, the more I fell in love. Discovering more about who he really was drew me closer to this man. We ate together, we walked in the park together, and we would sit and talk about the past; actually, he talked about his past. I listened and enjoyed every minute together. Everything was perfect. I didn't have to think about my life or my past issues. Often times, I could not believe this was my life. Finally, I met someone to overshadow the turmoil that often drowned my thoughts.

Weeks went by, and then months, and we still wanted to see each other. We continued to share our life stories, but at this point, I shared more about my past rather than only being on the listening end. I shared the church hurt and bad relationship experiences, and I felt as though I could talk to him about anything. We were becoming closer each day. This relationship was what I had been waiting for. I had a man who loved me and understood what it meant to place God first in my life, but to my surprise, this card was getting ready to play itself out.

After months of fun and good conversation, we decided to let the rest of the world in on our relationship. The time had come for him to meet my 16-year-old son, the second person who had my heart after God. I could not hold him back any longer, and I figured they would be great together! He has a son, and I hoped he would love my son, too. Sadly, these thoughts didn't pan out quite as

I thought. No one told me that men change and throw consistency out the window, and God knows that nobody ever said my son, my reason for living, would feel left out or as if I didn't pick the right man.

Lord knows, though, that my relationship went left after Kavon met my boyfriend.

Kavon and my boyfriend didn't see eye-to-eye. Their connection and communication were the worst of the worst. They truly did not want to share me. My man from heaven started to feel like the partner from hell. The card I had in my hand suddenly felt like a joker, and I wondered if God was anywhere to be found. I couldn't keep them together in the same room. That man that I loved did not seem to want my son around, and my son felt left out. I questioned whether or not this was the same man of God, the same loving and devoted father I had met several months ago.

"Who was this man?" I wondered, "And what happened to my son?"

As time went on, my feelings for my boyfriend began to fade, and the small issues became bigger. Waiting for my boyfriend to return to his old self had altered my love for him. The wait began to feel never-ending as if we reached the point of no return. He did not treat me the way he used to, and I was starting to feel like he wasn't looking at me as his future wife, the mother of his kids, or even worthy of being his devoted girlfriend. Instead, I felt like someone to pass the time with until he finds his next score. He started to come with a lot of let-me-downs, a lot of "no's," and his-way-or-no-way behaviors. Our relationship was changing in front of my eyes. I questioned if I heard God say this was unconditional love. The enjoyment I once had was slipping away from me. I expressed myself to him, over and over, but my words fell on deaf ears. I could hear God telling me it was over, but I resisted because I just did not want it to end. Every time he and I talked, he told me something about his past, his family, his issues, and his concerns, and I realized I was nowhere in the picture of his future. Our talks were nothing about me, us, or what the future held, but this was a pattern I accepted in the beginning and listening became the foundation of this one-sided relationship. I would listen to his hurts and pains while I kept my issues locked up inside. I was happy that he was a loving father and a great grandfather, but I did not seem to be part of his life in the same capacity. I was living with him while he lived in the past, fighting to come into the picture of the present. I found myself feeling alone, eating dinner at the table with him yet sitting in silence.

"Who am I to think that God would bless my mess?" I wondered.

I felt that I could have this perfect relationship without doing things God's way, and my fleshly feelings led me to believe I could fix everything if I pushed my way on God. God always works things out in our favor, but I had to understand that I needed Him to change my attitude in many areas within this relationship. My dream relationship was falling apart because I had my hand in so many different pots – my son, my love, my friends, and my family – all of which pulled me into different directions.

After praying for days and nights on end, listening to people say that my boyfriend is not meant to be my husband, and asking God if I am truly hearing Him correctly, I realized that God was not blessing this relationship. I also realized that if I tell people every bad thing I endure, I can't really expect them to support my relationship. Finally, I understood that this card God dealt me was designed to show me to *shut my mouth* and, instead, come to Him with my troubles, fears, feelings, and issues.

Oft times, we ask God to change situations or circumstances, but He can't because we have everyone else in the mix, and we find ourselves listening to them instead of His Word. At one point, I gave people the tools to use against me when it came to my relationship because I told them secrets and feelings that no one should have known.

Even my boyfriend couldn't appreciate my love for him because people were coming out of the woodwork, telling me about his past and asking if I really knew the type of man he was. I was told he was dangerous, and I fed into it, asking God to take him out of my life, but the love I developed for him caused me to draw closer to him in an unexplainable way. How is this the same man who allowed me to cry on his shoulder, time after time, and yet he turned so cold? Nevertheless, I told myself that I couldn't walk with God and do things my way at the same time. I had to let this man go. I had to give up my plans for our big wedding day.

    After I decided to walk away from him, my decision kept me up at night, tossing and turning, but I knew I had to stay away. Our relationship had finally come to an end. God told me that enough was enough, and I needed to play this card to reveal that he wasn't the one sent from God. All I could think was that I still wasn't married yet. I experienced another failed relationship, and my fear of being unwed crept into my mind. However, that fear didn't find a place of rest because I believed that God was working this out.

There were details of this story I deliberately excluded, however, some things are better left unsaid. This, yet another card.

Prayer

Lord God, I am sorry that I haven't trusted You in the areas that I should, especially involving my love life. God, sometimes it feels so hard to stop wanting to please my flesh by desiring a man in my life. I'm not sure if You see me love him more than You. God, I love You more than anything in the world, and I certainly don't want to disappoint You or ever make You feel that You are not right by my side. Understanding that You are a jealous God, I want to learn more and more about how things work when You allow couples to be married in the Kingdom. Lord, I see the things I have done wrong, and I should have come to You when I

Kayan Sykes

went to others, and for that, I am sorry. God, I love him, and I trust You will handle it from here. In Jesus' name, Amen.

5
The Trust Card

Trust is a firm belief in the reliability of someone or something. Many times, when looking up the meaning of trust, you realize that trust is created with someone. Trusting God is when you give Him your all, allow Him to take over your heart, and learn to lean not to your own understanding but toward the Bible to acknowledge Him in all His ways. When you learn to trust God, you lay it all down to give to Him – your fears, your concerns, your dreams, your hopes, your gratitude, and everything in between – and you do what He asks of you. When I think of this trust card, I see myself standing on the edge of whatever I am going through and falling back into His arms without fear or care in the world. I had to learn to trust God with my money, my child, my family, and my entire life. I used to ask myself questions like "Do you really trust God, and do you really trust yourself?"

Then, I dove further into the meaning of "trust" and researched how many times this word appears in the Bible because no one really talks about the importance of trust and how we can't walk with God without trusting Him with everything concerning our lives. Well, trust is mentioned 147 times in the Bible. Trust, in the Old Testament, is mentioned 134 times and 13 times in the New Testament.

Learning to be okay when God says "no" is a card in itself. God removed things from my life, and I learned to smile and keep moving, and that's largely because of trust. I used to cry my eyes out when life didn't go my way. I would question the Lord, and sometimes He wouldn't say a thing. The other times, He would softly nudge me to trust Him. It took losing my grandmother, my high school boyfriend, and my first husband, walking away from my salon, and almost losing my only son to realize God had my life under control on my behalf. Trusting God is hard, but once you learn to love God, you just let things go because, in the end, He will give it all back even better than before. I had experienced God move on my behalf when I knew things should not have worked out in my favor. I lost several jobs, yet God would open doors for me, time after time. When people could have killed me or thrown me in jail, God did not let those disasters happen, and when troubles arose, I trusted God because I knew He was in control.

Perspective is key.

When you trust God, you can look at misfortune from a different angle, knowing and believing He has great plans for your life. Trust is everything when it comes to God, and that can be a tough pill to swallow because when we strongly desire something and pray long and hard for that prayer to come to fruition, we may feel disappointed when we do not receive the answer or outcome we hoped for.

Faith, however, is not conditional.

God is worthy of trust and praise at all times. So, no matter how hard we pray or how badly we want something, God is not a genie in a bottle that merely grants a wish because that's what we requested. We must be willing to worship and testify regardless of increased favor and prosperity. As believers, we must acknowledge that although we pray for healing and favor, we may not receive what we wanted but that does not negate His power and sovereignty. Our trust should not be contingent upon the rate in which our prayers are answered. When we trust God with all of our hearts, we believe in the Miracle Worker, not the miracle that may come to pass. Something I love to remind myself is that I am blessed to trust such as a perfect Maker, yet I do not place my trust in Him simply to receive blessings.

There is a difference.

We are blessed to serve Him and trust Him, and it is our honor to walk in this trust-filled purpose.

♣

6

The Friend Card

When you think about the concept of friendship, you may associate it with someone who knows you better than you think you know yourself and a person who takes the position of caring about your interests at heart. Friends go above and beyond for each other. They are said to be someone you can talk to about anything and one who makes you comfortable sharing your most sacred thoughts. Some of the many traits we should have as a friend include being a good listener, trustworthy, dependability, honesty, and last but not the least, loyalty. I have a solid understanding of what friendship entails, and although I'm not claiming that I don't have these types of people around me, I am stating that God has become my number one.

Jesus had friends in the Bible, and we refer to those people as His disciples, such as we are today. We must check ourselves to make sure that we become the example given in His book and deal with each other as the disciples dealt with one another in which they deem friends. When I ask myself if I have been a good friend, such as Peter or Judas, the one who betrayed Jesus, my answer is typically no. I have not been a true friend to others, and I had to recognize this as my truth. It wasn't until God allowed me to go through tests and trials, and I found myself all alone, that I realized the people I had at the top of my list of friends would not go the extra mile for me.

Many times, I would talk to my friends about my life, and I found myself repeating some of the same tests yet falling into the same issues until I finally realized I was supposed to take my problems to God. I would pass Him and go to others, and trust me, that plan got me in a lot of trouble. I allowed others in my business, and then

I would have to hear their opinions about something they shouldn't have had access to, but that was my fault in the first place. Some of my friends and family would try to be there for me through my ups and downs, but there was only so much they could do. I would have to pull on God even more because I had to get them off my back and then ask Him to guide me through my problems as well as the add-on issues for opening up to the wrong ones.

  After feeling upset and lost, time and time again, I started to consult God and allow him to work out my issues. I lost friends when choosing not to place God first because He should have been the One, I consulted. I damaged relationships because I thought the person I considered a friend couldn't understand where I was coming from. I was placing a heavy weight on my friends, unknowingly expecting them to move mountains. When the only one who could handle that feat was and is God. I learned that not all friends could share in my pain or handle the pain I endured. After moving in the wrong direction, I became one of God's best friends, and I understood that He was already mine. Granted, I am not equal to God, as He is far wiser and more powerful than I could ever be but abiding by His guidance always works out for good, and He leads me the way a true friend would lead.

    I shared everything with God. Yes, even the stuff I knew was wrong and the stuff that I didn't exactly understand what I was feeling or doing. I started talking to Him about everything. I took Him to the worst events and the best ones as well. God became my go-to. He wouldn't always take my side, but He would reveal different sides of me, sides I needed to know and learn. I learned to look in the mirror and demand change for my life. I thought this friend card was to show me how my so-called friends had wronged me, but I was all wrong. This card was all about how I had wronged God. I put him second, time after time, and as time went by, I realized this card was for me to pick up, play, and never put down. After dealing with my many unfavorable situations, I understood that God would step back and wait for the very friends

I put all my trust in to disappoint me. So, I would have to come right back to Him. In my time of pain and anger, I would feel Him whisper, "Why did you go to them about that problem? I'm in control." In time, I learned to seek Him in every situation, no longer placing anyone or anything above His everlasting wisdom and grace.

Choosing God as your best friend is the best decision you could ever make because He will teach you the meaning of joy and love, and He will free you from harmful habits and destructive thoughts. He is the ultimate listener, and He will aid you during times of trouble. Best of all, God offers His gift of everlasting life, and there is absolutely nothing or no one that could compare to Him in the friendship department. You have a friend in Him; all you need to do is seek and accept.

Kayan Sykes

7

The Race Card

Race is a frequently discussed subject among the masses, rightfully involving strong feelings and opinions, yet we must remember that God never said He loved anyone more than another. We are all one in God's eyes. The Bible says "... and there before me was a great multitude that no one could count, from every nation, tribe, people and language, standing before the throne and before the Lamb" (Revelation 7:9 NIV). Many may disagree, but I have come to realize that we could all treat each other with more love and respect. I was blessed to have been raised in a diverse environment, having attended a Lutheran school and then a public school among a mixture of people who I have come to know and love. God showed me cultural differences at a young age because He knew where my life was headed and that I would need a broad understanding of people and respective cultural differences. He knew I would have to deal with all types of people and, hopefully, see them in the same way He sees us – as children of Christ. Please believe, I'm still human and, admittedly, I've believed stereotypes as much as the next person, but I also accept the Word and how God wants us to love one another as we love ourselves.

    Nevertheless, facing cultural differences and trying to gain a better understanding of the people we interact with, whether once in a while or on a day-to-day basis, is so much more than dealing with matters of race. Human interaction is a continual test from God. He wants to see if we are not only reading His Word but applying these scriptures to our lives. Ultimately, He wants us to have a Christ-like heart. So, we must love our neighbor at all times, but in that commandment comes a challenge – a challenge He knows we will face because not everyone we meet is full of rainbows and butterflies. Thankfully, we are equipped with His Word, love, and mercy, and I know I can take on the day with those tools in my spiritual belt.

Being in the position to deal with countless different people on a daily basis at my place of employment, I've developed a strong understanding of human interaction. Although I've learned to understand people, I remain challenged to love them as He loves us. Nevertheless, as a believer, that is a challenge I am ready to accept and face. As God opened doors for me, He surely showed me how he was guiding me to find my way out of many challenging situations. With time, He opened more doors of opportunity and led me to attain a position at a five-star spa and salon where I would encounter every ethnicity known to man. Many days, I questioned God, because dealing with certain problematic customers definitely wasn't what I signed up for.

Do I really have to be treated this way?

Why are You forcing me to keep a good face and a closed mouth?

Why am I dealing with this?

As much as I would keep a soft voice and customer-service-geared attitude, I continued to encounter rudeness, disrespect, and misplaced anger. Although challenging, I learned to save face in those trying moments, dealing with the same people who claim to love God but treat me and others in the ways the Word advises against. There are moments I want to breakdown and cry, wishing we were one instead of divided groups, but I continue to hear God's voice saying that He wants me to remember a soft word turns away wrath (Proverbs 15:1). My mind remains on God, and rather than exchanging rudeness, I respond as a child of God and move on with my day, saving myself a lot of frustration. We must remember that all we do is unto God, and the reason I work at this particular place is because that is where God wants me at this time. This card was dealt for me and only me, the same way you have a set of cards exclusive to your life.

Even though there are days I fail at doing it all right, I continue to try until I get it right; I can't stop until I fulfill my purpose, and this purpose is heavily weighted in my interactions with others, whether or not I am doing the work of His Kingdom. We cannot read the Bible yet have an everyday life that goes against His Word. The Bible is meant to be read and used in accordance with our lives. We are to take these biblical principles and apply them to our lives, whether at our job, the grocery store, or walking down the street. We have to love our neighbor, and we must live our lives in a way that pleases God. Otherwise, we will succumb to our fleshly desires, only to expand the devil's territory.

Playing the race card can easily take us out of our Godly element, because people do not always treat one another with respect, especially in today's society when tensions seem more escalated than ever before. However, we must remember that we are equally created in the image of God, and our purpose is to glorify Him while we are on this Earth. We must do our part so that everyone lives in peace and harmony, and if your actions and words are not in accordance with His image, then you need to play your card in such a way that pleases God and His Will for harmony.

8

The Dream Card

Sleeping to dream is an amazing feeling. Not only do we rest our bodies, but during that time of slumber, we have a series of unique thoughts. Sometimes, we wake up and remember our dreams; other times, we are completely unsure of what we dreamt. Dreams are important in reference to the Bible, too. The more we read the Bible, the more these scriptures and verses are embedded in our minds, and since our dreams are often based on our subconscious, it's best to fill our subconscious with Biblical thoughts. "A dream comes through much activity," as stated in Ecclesiastes 5:3, thus sharing that our dreams are a result of our thoughts, conversations, and interactions. I like to look at this verse as a subtle reminder to direct our thoughts and energy toward the Lord so that my stimuli is aligned with the Word.

Like you, I've had countless dreams, some I remember more vividly than others. I've dreamt of being with someone or that I was in a specific place, and almost every one of those dreams has come to pass in one way or another. Nineteen years ago, when I walked by Kavon's father, I said I would dream of having his baby. Yes, he was good-looking, but beyond that, I truly had no idea he would be the father of my child. Well, here I am today, sharing this book of which Kavon's family is intertwined with.

We must be mindful of our thoughts.

Our thoughts become our actions.

I have done this a lot in my life, speaking something for it to turn into reality, yet not knowing that God had my next move already planned. Often, we think God is not listening, or He doesn't hear us, but He knows, sees, feels, and hears all, and He gives us dreams as a small sign to let us know the power of His presence. I've received His messages through dreams, and I take these messages seriously. As believers, we must guard our hearts and minds, making sure not to expose ourselves to a potentially unwanted dream. God reminds us of this valuable lesson in Philippians 4:8:

> "Finally, brethren, whatever things are true, whatever things are noble, whatever things are just, whatever things are pure, whatever things are lovely, whatever things are of good report, if there is any virtue, and if there is anything praiseworthy – meditate on these things."

Although I've had my fair share of nightmares, I'm grateful for the peaceful dreams He has given me, and I have chosen to step out on faith and try to live those dreams, too.

As you go through life, you learn to step out on faith. Sometimes, you have to make decisions that people may not understand, but their understanding is not your concern because we know, as believers, that God has a unique way of showing us signs, love, and a promise for a better tomorrow. Tap into your dreams, and dream with faith. I've played the dream card, many times, and many times this has worked because I was willing to trust God and take leaps of faith. Admittedly, I wasn't always as spiritual as I should have been, but I tried God at His Word. All it took was faith the size of a mustard seed (Matthew 17:20).

If the Bible said that God healed and delivered the people, then why wouldn't He do the same for you?

It's been my experience to dream the impossible and watch God bring it to pass. You have to dream whatever your heart desires, and you have to do the work required to see it come to pass. Pray without ceasing, fast, and believe you will receive. Ask, and doors will open. God will give it to you, and if He does not grant your dream, it's strictly because He has bigger plans for your life than what you envisioned. He is not a genie but a God of purpose and intention.

I've always told myself to trust God. I figure that trusting God is much more peaceful and rewarding than feeding my fears. I close my eyes and envision falling into God's arms, allowing Him to catch me. Trust me, dreaming big requires courage, but with God's help, you can do the impossible. I could not have written this book about my life if I did not have big dreams of what life could truly be, and I could not have executed this task without God's mercy.

Don't get me wrong – having courage, following through on my dreams, and manifesting the Word have not always been easy, and as you have read, I've had many tests and trials. I've also fought with God along the way and wanted life to go according to my plan, but when I aligned with His Word, my dreams put me right back in place. I've cried rivers of tears in my day, and although those situations hurt like hell, I am comforted by the fact that God saw every one of my tears, just like he sees yours, and He wants nothing more than for us to give Him our pain, worries, and fears. My pain pushed me to learn how to lean on God for help. I was hurt, broken, and all of the above, but I never stopped dreaming for more. I found peace in my dreams. I took my power back from Satan when he would tell me I was crazy, and life would never pan out. Instead, I dreamed bigger. You must tell yourself you are a dreamer with purpose, a dreamer with power, and a dreamer under God.

♣

9
The Vegas Card

As I look back over my life, I understand why God removed me from certain situations and took people out of my life. I believe I was on a stage, singing and standing in a position I never wanted to really to be in. I used to say that I did not like people, but what I came to understand is that I did, in fact, love others. I just did not want them to see my flaws. Instead, I wanted to be alone. I would often wonder why I could not muster up the courage to be more upfront like everyone else. At a young age, I told myself that my fears never allowed me to step out on courage. Nevertheless, I began to develop despite my fears, the people who tried to jump in front of me, and those who did not guide me toward achieving my best... but God! He had to show me that those people could not provide my needs, and it would take Him and only Him to place me just where I need to be; they surely couldn't place me where they didn't know I belonged.

When I moved to Las Vegas, I had a friend who made remarks that made me question myself. Clearly, she wasn't a friend, but at the time, I wanted to believe I made a new friend in this new, unfamiliar place. There were several times she told me I was slow or stupid. Don't get me wrong – there were times she uplifted me, but there were many other times when she put me down.

"I just want to carry your Bible," she encouraged in one breath, only to shout cruel remarks in the next. "Leave me alone before I tell you what I really think about you." Now, with wisdom and clarity, I understand this toxic friendship was all in God's plan. I experienced these hurtful remarks and dysfunctional friendship, only to develop my wisdom and strength, now knowing to make better relationship decisions and exercise more self-love.

Recently, my pastor spoke straight to me and my situation during a Sunday service. I couldn't believe my ears, as I was just at the breaking point of trying to figure out how I'm going to pay my bills, keep my car, and manage Kavon and the journey ahead, yet God did just that in placing this sermon on my ears and heart during such a crucial time. With all of the hell I've been through and the pain I've suffered, one would think that my child and I would have given up by now, and as I type this and reflect on our journey, I remember time after time when life seemed bleak, yet I'm comforted by His promise, grace, and mercy. I remember pulling my car up to my house that I was renting from a family member. We did not have heat, nor did we have beds. Instead, Kavon and I slept on the floor. We then moved into an apartment, now having a bed that was purchased during a prior relationship, but my ex-boyfriend took back the bed that my son was sleeping on. I cried my eyes out because in that very apartment I, again, had no gas, no warm showers, and no sign of a better tomorrow.

"How could I go through this again?" I cried aloud.

We ended up moving to Texas, and for two months, we struggled to belong in a home that was not exactly welcoming, as I shared in a previous chapter.

"Lord, when is my change coming?" I questioned, desperately hoping for an immediate answer yet knowing that God doesn't exactly work like that.

Despite the pain, you could look into my eyes and know that God has truly blessed me to be in a place where I'm confident in following him, no matter where we go. I'm so grateful to know that God has put me in a position that many people want to be in, and that is a space of unbreakable faith, regardless of circumstances. Although there was a point when I felt as if God did me wrong because I wasn't married, I learned that God does not punish; He teaches. God does not cause pain; He causes growth. He uses our pain and stepping stones for elevation, and I am eternally grateful to have received a mere fraction of His infinite wisdom.

Never forget this – God loves the sinner, not the sin. No matter the sin, each one hurts God's heart equally. Regardless of the sin, He wants you to turn from your wicked ways and do what is right in His eyes. Consider the lifestyle you are living and go to God and change your ways. I know that it's easier said than done. Trust me, I've had to do the same, and only then did life start to work out a bit better. Honesty and reflection are key to growth. If you do not acknowledge your sins, repent, and strive for better, you are doomed to repeat your mistakes. Thankfully, I've been fortunate to take this wisdom with me into adulthood and apply it to several different situations.

There is a young man at work whom I really enjoy working with. He's considerably younger, but he's a wonderful coworker that I like talking to and working alongside. Great coworkers always make a job ten times more enjoyable, right? I pray for this young man often, especially because he has shared his pain with me. He told me that he attended an all-boys' school and that he liked his experience of being in the locker room. He told me that he realized he was different, that he had a girlfriend who hurt him, and that he did not enjoy having sex with her. As a result, his mind went to a dark place. As he shared his deepest pains and thoughts with me, I realized that we all have experiences that have hurt us, and those experiences may very well be different, yet how we react to escape the pain is how we differ.

"Are you uncomfortable working with me?" he randomly asked me one day.

"Not at all," I replied. "I enjoy working with you, but when I tell you I am praying for you, I'm sharing that with you to help you, not judge you. It's not my job to judge you."

I meant what I said to him because I wholeheartedly believe that I'm supposed to show others my light, often through prayer, and that's exactly what I'm going to do for others.

He smiled, and our differences did not seem to matter at that moment because he felt the power of my words and the strength of my prayers. When he smiled, I realized that I went from being a girl who used to sleep in the front row of my uncle's service, Sunday after Sunday, to a person who enjoys church and happily shares the Word with others.

I remember the day, many years ago, when my mother told me that God had called me to sing. My uncle would say that God told me to use what I have. I didn't fully understand that those words would change my life once I applied them through worship. At the time, I figured I might as well help my family and participate in the choir. In participating in choir, I also began to attention Life Class on Thursday nights. My uncle would put down the Bible, and we would ask questions which helped us from one service to the next. Developing an active church life was the best thing that ever happened to me, ultimately positioning me for situations to help others, just like the moment I shared with my coworker. Through an active church life, I truly learned to live, be saved, and gain a better understanding of this "church thing." Even though I had been in church all my life, I entered a new season of really changing my life for the good.

During this time, we developed a group of women who would share their life stories. I suddenly felt as though I wasn't alone. I would learn the Word on Thursday night, and by Sunday, miracles would happen because my heart and mind were shifting according to His Word. We started traveling with the church, and life was going pretty good, but as time progressed, the enemy got mad. The enemy always gets mad when the attention shines on God instead of him.

The separation of our family grew stronger, and the devil played his hand so well that it became hard to celebrate God. In those weak moments, when we foolishly succumb to the devil's workings, we begin to doubt who we are singing about and who we are learning about in Life Class. Everyone has their own idea of what God wants them to do, but if we could have been on one-accord, our mission at church would have worked out. Instead, I saw families fighting other families in the church. People seemingly forgot the purpose of service. As a young woman, I did not understand the depth of the situation, but these battles began to play out in my face as I entered adulthood.

When brothers and sisters are against each other, no longer praying for each other and using their light to illuminate others, it takes me back to the Cane and Abel story in the Bible.

Are we not our brother's keeper?

In the Bible, we read about when Cain killed his brother and lied about it. As I have mentioned, I have learned that God shows us how to handle situations in our everyday lives by using examples from His Word. When life unfolds, we really shouldn't find these occurrences to be strange. Instead, we should go back and learn from His examples. There is an answer to every problem if only we look in the Bible. I wish I had learned these lessons before because life would have been so much easier. You know how the saying goes, though – when you know better, you do better.

When our church family was falling apart, we were not being one another's keeper. Maybe it's safe to say we hadn't read the Word in a similar fashion or we had yet to have a full understanding that God gives us different gifts, dispositions, and ways of pleasing Him. Instead of knowing and using all the special ways He created us, we allowed jealousy to overtake our bond. God will favor us depending on our sacrifices to Him, but we must accept that He gave everyone something of importance. God blesses everyone, but we must be sure to give our all to Him, every chance we can, and trust that He will turn our circumstances around. If you have a wonderful skill set or talent, more advanced than your brother or sister, do not tear them down. Instead, join together and help them in every way you can in an effort to build His Kingdom.

I've asked God many, many questions, only to find out that He was counting on me to act differently. There is a common example of the oldest child doing something better than the younger, but thanks unto God that no one was killed in the flesh, yet words have been spoken to kill the spirit of each of them. Between the unfolding and rebuilding of my church family and the countless different people I've encountered in life, including my beloved work friend, we are called to love one another, not harm, judge, or criticize. Look at your family and think back to when you have witnessed a breakdown in that relationship. Make a promise to stop this behavior and change it today. Let's help our brothers and sisters in the way of love and work together to reach a place in which God would be pleased. Let's empower our brothers and sisters to access His favor in the same manner you may have. We have to understand that all parties have to be willing vessels. God wants to use all of us, and He has given us the power to pray and believe in His great Works.

Kayan Sykes

10

The End Card

As the days pass, and I grow older, I'm starting to understand my purpose on a grander scale and how my purpose ties together in different areas of my life and the lives of others. When I think back to the ups and downs and rights and wrongs, I realize that a runner never stops running until they reach the point of no return or their final destination. I envision my final card as a place where I dreamed of being, a place on the mountaintop of my faith. By the grace of God, I've reached happiness in a place where no man could ever take it away from me. I pray you find the same level of happiness, too.

Never stop.

Never give up.

Never throw in the towel.

Kayan Sykes

Just hold onto God's loving hand.

I pray that this book demonstrates the power of faith, despite circumstances, and I can truly say that God has blessed me, and I am going to run the course and see where He takes me until my final hour. Those closest to me often advised that I ensure I was following God's instructions. Sure enough, I was following the right path, and I knew this path was on par with His Will for my life because I was very much in tune with His Word. Never listen to people instead of your gut feeling. That gut feeling is a gift from God – it's the gift of discernment.

Writing from a place of peace and honesty instead of bitterness and lies is empowering. I live in a free place, knowing God has put me in position to dream, and my Faith in Him is unbelievable, on an all-time high. There was a time when I felt as if God had done me wrong. I know, I know – the One who always has my back, yet I dared to think He was my enemy, but hey – growth is beautiful, and through this realization, no matter how shameful, I was able to grow in faith and have a heart of Christ. Because I wasn't married, and life seemed so good for others who did follow His divine order, I assumed I was being punished.

When my child told me that he wanted to leave from the home we were currently living in, I wanted to crumble. The next morning, after I had made it home from work, all of his belongings were gone, and I felt like I wanted to die.

When the man I loved stopped answering his phone and started dating another woman despite telling me that we were going to get back together, I released my final cry. "God, I have played these cards, and I can't play them anymore. Lord, I can't play this hand you have dealt me!"

But God!

The power of prayer is mighty, and this shifted my entire being. Happiness is something I never felt would come my way, but to God be the glory, my life is full of joy, and I started to love myself through the eyes of Christ.

The devil would tell me to end my life, many times, but I didn't. He urged me to give up. He wanted me to stay angry with God, yet every second I invested in His Word to refute the devil's evil workings was well worth my time. I vowed to God that if I'm going to be alone for the rest of my days, I am going to be happy. I have reached a place of salvation, and I have learned it well. I want what He wants me to have, and nothing else.

I pray you learn from this book.

I pray you walk away from this text and feel strongly about God's love, power, and Will for your life.

Life has many ups and downs, and we have to learn to depend on God for everything. I will never stop playing God's card. He dealt me this hand for a reason, and I will play this set of cards until the day I die. I have so much more work to do in the name of His Kingdom, and this book is just the first step.

Today is the beginning of a brand-new life!

About the Author

Kayan Sykes is a 44-year old divorced mother of one 19-year-old son, with plenty of life experiences! Born in Saint Louis, Missouri she was raised in the Pentecostal Church. Sykes has been on the journey with God nearly 30 years. Sykes believes God is the very best thing that has ever happen to her! In the midst of intense trial, Sykes attributes God as being her true anchor. Sykes worked as a hairstylist for nearly 20 years, using her gift to help women feel great about themselves in every way and has now completed her first book! Currently, Sykes resides in Las Vegas, NV.

Kayan Sykes

The Hand God Dealt Me

Notes/Reflections

Kayan Sykes

www.ingramcontent.com/pod-product-compliance
Lightning Source LLC
Chambersburg PA
CBHW071217160426
43196CB00012B/2336